D1177549

AJANTA AND ELLORA

Text by
Leila Ghosh and Dalia Roy

IBH

CLB 1656
World marketing rights with India Book House PVT. Ltd.,
412 Tulsani Chambers, 212 Backbay Reclamation,
Nariman Point, Bombay 400 021, India.
© 1986 Illustrations and text: Colour Library Books Ltd.,
   Guildford, Surrey, England.
Text filmsetting by Acesetters Ltd., Richmond, Surrey, England.
Printed and bound in Barcelona, Spain by Cronion, S.A.
All rights reserved.
ISBN 0 86283 498 8

In the vast, untamed wilderness of the Indian sub-continent numerous mysteries and wonders are still being explored and unearthed. One of the more dramatic revelations of the nineteenth century involved the now famous caves of Ajanta and Ellora, in Maharashtra state. They were discovered quite accidentally, after centuries of oblivion, by the keen eye of a British hunter. His subsequent excavations revealed a world of great beauty, and brought to light and to life a most ancient and august civilisation. In that civilisation an art culture inspired by spiritual fervour became a way of religious life. Popular devotion to the three quite distinct contemporary religions found ready expression through the most spectacular art forms that transcended barriers of time and language then, as now.

Discovered in 1819, the caves and their treasury of paintings date from about 200 BC to just prior to the expulsion of Buddhism from India (about AD 650) and its replacement by Brahmanism. The Ajanta Caves, about 100km from the town of Aurangabad, are entirely Buddhist, and their illustrations recount the life of Lord Buddha both before his renunciation of the pleasures of the world and in his enlightened phase. Wall paintings, executed in long, impressive sweeps, are still vivid in their original vibrant colours and fascinating in their minute detail.

Cut into the scarp of a cliff, the caves – they number some thirty in all – are either chapels (charityas) or monasteries (viharas). All were structured in such a way that a flood of natural light poured into them, while at the same time their devout inhabitants were adequately protected from extremes of heat or cold. A stream flows down the ravines in the cliffs and ends abruptly in a series of seven waterfalls (Sat Kund) of which the last forms a drop of 70 or 80 feet, and the entire complex of caves, seen from exterior viewpoints, is enchantingly picturesque.

All the caves are numbered for ease of reference both for students and for everyday visitors. The most awe-inspiring of the paintings are to be found in the caves numbered 1, 2, 16 and 17.

About 33kms from Aurangabad stands a large, crescent-shaped hill which contains the rock-hewn temples and monasteries of Ellora. These are comprised of thirteen Mayahana Buddhist, sixteen Hindu and five Jain caves. The most noteworthy are numbers 10 and 12 (Buddhist), 14, 15 and 16 (Hindu) and 33 (Jain). While it is true that, architecturally, the Ellora Caves differ from those at Ajanta – since they have front courtyards and entrances through the outer wall of the rock – their sculptures are just as absorbing and eloquent as Ajanta's paintings. The most remarkable of the shrines is the Kailasha Temple, standing 50 metres long and 33 metres wide. By a marvel of physical endurance and persistence, it was chiselled by hand from a single, massive rock to include a gateway, pavilion, courtyard, vestibule, sanctum and tower. In fact, the masons started building from the top of the mountain and worked downwards, thus cleverly eliminating the need for scaffolding.

In the galleries are recreated the heroic myths about Lord Shiva fighting against the forces of Evil. Although the carvings at Ellora are the work of devotees of three separate religions, the structural patterns, probably dictated by the demands of the rock formation, have a great deal in common. Nevertheless, it is obvious even to the most casual observer that the Jain temples are distinctly ascetic in tone, whereas the Hindu and Buddhist are outrageously sensuous and virile. In this connection it should be explained that the Buddhist art forms, though essentially austere and self-disciplined, had by then become influenced by the rich, almost irresistible imagery of Brahman culture.

A visit to these wonders of art and architecture is not complete without taking the additional time to look around Aurangabad – the inevitable base for all visitors. The town's towering, sprawling, 12th-century Daulatabad Fort, the ancient watermill at Panchakki, the Aurangabad Caves and the Bibika Maqbara, that Taj-like mausoleum built by the Moghul King Aurangeb as an immortal gift to his wife, serve as perfect accompaniments to the feast of delights which Ajanta and Ellora offer.

But the contrast between the urban attractions and the serenity of the caves is more than impressive. For at these remote sites, secluded from an outside world of frenetic activity, a pervading monastic calm and inner certainty prevail – a suitable reflection of the fact that the important aspect of Indian art which they contain reached the zenith of its development through deep and abiding spiritual inspiration.

The Yakshi Ambika (previous page), seated on her lion under a mango tree, was carved during the
9th or 10th century in the Jain Cave 32 at Ellora. Facing page: a seated Buddha, Ellora.

Facing page: the balanced facade and large chaitya window of Cave 9, an early chaitya (Buddhist shrine or chapel) excavated at Ajanta in the 1st century B.C. The arched form of the chaitya window, based on the shape of the leaf of the bodhi tree beneath which the Buddha attained nirvana, is repeated above the portico of Cave 19 (this page), an elaborate, 5th-century Ajanta shrine.

Carved out of the solid rock, the caves of Ajanta are the work of generations of Buddhist monks. Their excavations began in the 2nd century B.C. and, continuing over a period of 800 years, produced a complex of five chaityas (shrines) and 25 viharas (monasteries), executed with incredible patience and skill and hallowed with numerous images of the Buddha (these pages).

Cave No. 19 (these pages) at Ajanta is a fully developed chaitya excavated in the 5th century during the Gupta period, the golden age of Buddhist art. This page: buddhas beside the chaitya's entrance, and (facing page) its tall, elaborate stupa. Stupas, enshrining the ashes of a Buddhist saint or teacher, were early centers of Buddhist pilgrimage, and, in miniature versions, came to form the culmination of the chaitya.

The caves of Ajanta are carved from the rock of a steep, semicircular scarp (facing page bottom) in the Indhyari Hills, overlooking the Waghara River. Facing page: (top) the narrow, richly-carved verandah of Cave 1, a vihara, and (this page) the stupa of Cave 26, a chaitya, both excavated in the 6th-century by Mahayana Buddhist monks.

The murals in caves 1 and 2 at Ajanta were painted during the Gupta period (320-650), when Buddhist art flourished. These pages: the interpretation of Queen Maya's dream, a scene from the story of the birth of the Buddha, Cave 2. Overleaf: (left) the still-clear colours of ceiling decoration, and (right) richly-jewelled ladies in Cave 1.

The theme of the thousand buddhas, used in the wall decoration of the Cave 2 vihara (these pages), Ajanta, celebrates the Miracle of Shravasti, when Buddha took the form of a thousand celestial buddhas in order to confound a heretic.

These pages: King Mahajanaka takes leave of his queen, an episode of the Mahajanaka jataka in Cave 1, and (overleaf) the pandit Vidhura, another incarnation of the bodhisattva, instructs the serpent king in the buddhist dharma in a jataka depicted on the walls of Cave 2, Ajanta.

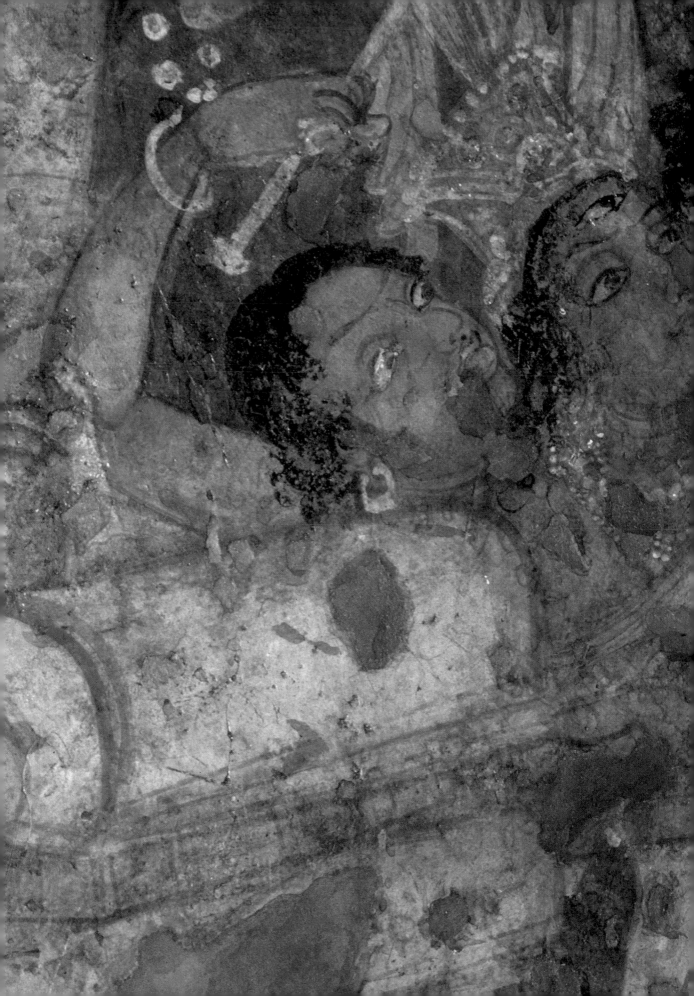

These pages: the infant Buddha held by one of three figures – possibly the Hindu gods Brahma, Vishnu and Shiva –, his mother Maya standing holding the branch of a tree, part of a mural depicting the birth of Buddha in Cave 2, Ajanta. Overleaf: details of contemporary courtly styles and adornments, Ajanta.

The sturdy pillars and (above) the sculpture of Gajantaka, an aspect of the Hindu god Shiva, in Cave 29, or the Dumar Lena, at Ellora. A shrine dedicated to Shiva, Cave 29 was excavated during the 5th to 6th centuries under the patronage of the Vakataka dynasty.

Facing page: carved in the rock of 5th-century Cave 21, the Ramesvara cave at Ellora, the ten-headed demon-king Ravana shakes Mount Kailasa, on which sit the unconcerned god Shiva and Parvati, his bride. This page: the facade of Cave 10, known as the Visvarkarma or Carpenter's Cave, its trefoil window flanked by groups of flying figures.

The Kailasanatha Temple (these pages) at Ellora, designated Cave 16, is dedicated to the Hindu god Shiva. The vast temple dates from A.D. 765 and was cut from the hillside under the patronage of King Krishna I of the Rashtrakuta dynasty.

These pages and overleaf: the courtyard, porch and main hall, or mandapa, of the Kailasanatha Temple at Ellora. Three great trenches were cut into the hillside, and the intricate complex of the temple hewn out of the resulting solid block, each section being cut, sculpted and polished before the workers moved down to the next. It took over a hundred years to complete.

Probably a symbol of King Krishna I, the patron of the Kailasanatha Temple, the pillar in the left-hand section of its courtyard (these pages) stands fifty feet high. Remains of the white stucco which once faced the entire complex are still visible.

The central shrine (these pages) of Ellora's Cave 29, dedicated to Shiva, is guarded on all four sides by massive door guardians. Overleaf: (left top) the marriage of the Hindu god Shiva with Parvati, the four-headed god Brahma acting as officiating priest, and (left bottom) seated Buddhas in one of Ellora's twelve Buddhist caves. (Right top) the elegant balcony and facade of Buddhist Cave 10, and (right bottom) goddesses, Ellora.

Cave 32 at Ellora dates from c1100 and is dedicated to Mahavira, the last of the 24 saints of Jainism. The great lotus (previous pages left) carved on its ceiling symbolises enlightenment, while the tree growing around the legs of the Jain saint Gomeshavara (these pages), who guards the cave's main shrine, represents the cosmic knowledge and paradisical state of the enlightened being. Previous pages right: the posture of perfection.

This page: the image of Mahavira in the main shrine of the Jain Cave 32, Ellora, with his emblem, the lion, beneath him. Facing page: (top) the facade of Cave 32, and (bottom) statuary damaged by weathering and desecration, Ellora. Overleaf: carvings, (left top) of Gajantaka, an aspect of Shiva, in Cave 29, (left bottom) of Ravana shaking Mount Kailasa, Cave 21, and (right) of Matanga Yaksha, a further form of Shiva, on his elephant in Cave 32, Ellora.

Previous pages: (left top) elephants shower Gaja Lakshmi, the goddess of prosperity, as she welcomes devotees to the Kailasanatha Temple at Ellora, and (left bottom) an elephant, symbol of dignity and strength, guards the entrance to Cave 32. (Right top) the central shrine of Cave 29, and (bottom) evidence of the paint and plaster work with which many of Ellora's rock sculptures were once finished. These pages: the rocky cliff into which the caves of Ellora are cut.

Previous pages: (right top) the courtyard, (left) caryatid elephants supporting the main temple or mandapa, and (right bottom) scenes from the Ramayana on the plinth of the mandapa, Kailasanatha Temple, Ellora. Facing page: lions on the mandapa roof, and (this page) the lotus shikara or spire, of Kailasanatha Temple.

Ellora's Cave 10 is both a chaitya, with rounded stupa (facing page), and a vihara, in which Buddhist monks lived in cells added to the courtyard and balcony. The chaitya ceiling is barrel-vaulted in imitation of the wooden rafters of early, brick-built chaityas. This page: formidable guards protect the central shrine of Shiva in Cave 29, Ellora.

These pages: caryatid elephants supporting the mandapa of Kailasanatha Temple, Ellora. Overleaf: (left) weathered carving of Gajanataka, Ellora, (right) seated Buddha beneath a heavy overhang, and (following pages) a shrine in the courtyard of Cave 32, Ellora.